# Take up
# Gymnastics

## Take up Sport

Titles in this series currently available or shortly to be
published:

# Take up Gymnastics

Principal contributor:

**Barry Benn**

Honorary BAGA National Coach
and Gymnastics Development Officer for the
City of Birmingham

SPRINGFIELD BOOKS LIMITED

Copyright © Springfield Books Limited and White Line Press
1989

ISBN 0 947655 62 X

First published 1989 by
**Springfield Books Limited**
Springfield House, Norman Road, Denby Dale, Huddersfield
HD8 8TH

Edited, designed and produced by
**White Line Press**
60 Bradford Road, Stanningley, Leeds LS28 6EF

Editors: Noel Whittall and Philip Gardner
Design: Krystyna Hewitt
Diagrams: Barry Benn

Printed and bound in Great Britain

**Photographic credits**
Supersport: cover photographs, and pages 6, 9, 10, 22, 44,
    47, 48, 49, 50, 51(2), 52, 53, 54
All other photographs by Barry Benn

**Acknowledgements**
Our thanks to the gymnasts who appear in the instructional
photographs: Rebecca Aucott, Katie Bird, Rachel Burgess,
Shulay Crane, Ian Greenhill, Germaine Gregory, Katie
Henderson, Lisa Iommi, Leonie Prentice, Claire Scobie and
David Williams; and to the coaches: Phil Barrow and Tansin
Benn.

# Contents

*Champion British gymnasts Lisa Elliott and Ian Shelley*

# 1

# Introduction

Gymnastics consists of performing exercises with a mixture of muscular control and artistic grace. Throughout history, there has been an unbroken tradition of people taking part in gymnastics both as a sport and as an entertainment. This goes right back to the original Olympic Games in the great days of ancient Greece.

Many children have a natural instinct for gymnastics, and don't need encouragement from adults to get started. Look in any park, garden or school playground, and there will be children turning cartwheels, playing leap-frog, balancing along the tops of walls or rolling down grassy banks. This voluntary enthusiasm is not confined to children: given half a chance, many adults will perform handstands too, as a few minutes spent at your local leisure pool will show!

Even at the most basic level there is great pleasure in learning these skills and then performing them more and more competently. There is also a natural desire to move on to more difficult and complicated exercises. *Take up Gymnastics* will help you to master gymnastics skills in a progressive manner, and to guide children safely towards extending their performance range.

The world of gymnastics is so diverse that it offers something for everyone. This introduction might lead you into artistic gymnastics, sports acrobatics, rhythmic or recreational gymnastics. You will join the millions of people who gain a great deal of pleasure and sense of achievement from a sport which can easily remain a lifelong source of satisfaction.

# 2

# Getting started

Television coverage of Olympic events has given modern gymnastics a tremendous boost since the early 1970s, and the sport is now a very popular recreational activity. Here are the main things to look for when seeking a gym club for yourself or your children:

● Good coaches or teachers. Check that there will *always* be someone in charge with proper qualifications. The standard of supervision must be high: really good instruction and training are essential if gymnastics is to be learned safely.

● Good equipment. It does not have to be new, provided that it is well maintained. If floor mats are fraying around the edges, or there are splinters on the benches, then the standard of instruction is unlikely to be good either.

● A warm gymnasium. Flexibility of the body is an important feature of gymnastics, and you cannot be fully flexible when cold.

● Regular sessions. You need to build your skills steadily: there's no point in having a burst of activity and then doing no gymnastics for the next week or two.

## Safety

All active games and sports carry some risk of injury, so it is important that precautions are taken to make the risk as small as possible without taking the fun away. In gymnastics you must make sure that:

● your body is prepared for the activities you wish to practise or learn

● you are suitably dressed (see page 11)

● you understand exactly what it is you are trying to achieve and follow the necessary learning stages

**2**

*Skilled coaching is essential to learn gymnastics safely.*

- any apparatus that you use is suitable and in good condition
- you learn your gymnastics under the supervision of a qualified teacher or coach. While a few gymnastics skills may be learned safely without assistance, guidance is essential to ensure that you learn at the right speed and that you practise safely and with the correct technique.

## Where to find a club

School is the obvious starting-point for most young gymnasts. Do not rule out this possibility even if your school has no gym club: often the teacher in charge at a nearby school with a club will admit keen learners.

Your local sport and leisure centre may well offer classes in gymnastics. If there is not a class suitable for you, try the local leisure services department, or enquire at the library.

The courses at leisure centres tend to be aimed at recreational gymnastics rather than competition. If you are more interested in competing, then a true gymnastics club will be the best choice. In Great Britain, you will be able to get a list of all the clubs in your area if you contact the secretary of your regional gymnastics association through your local Sports Council office. Most other countries have a national gymnastics association which will be able to provide similar information.

## Physical preparation

Every gymnastics skill requires a certain amount of strength and suppleness if it is to be done safely and correctly. For example, it would be silly to try to do a handstand before you are strong enough to take your weight on your hands — you first have to concentrate on other activities which will develop your arms. Once you have the strength, you also need suppleness: you won't be able to hold an absolutely straight handstand if you are stiff in the shoulders. As you approach each new skill, look carefully at the physical demands that it will make on you, and ask your teacher or coach if you are ready to learn it.

Some of the of the exercises shown further on in this book will help you to prepare yourself correctly.

# Equipment and apparatus

Good matting is essential. When you are learning a skill, you may need to practise many times before you master it. Thin or hard matting will make practice uncomfortable and can cause strains or bruising, while frayed edges to mats are likely to trip you up.

Most of the gymnastics skills you learn as a beginner require only the simplest of apparatus. Whatever you use must be in a safe condition. Apart from the obvious dangers from old apparatus which may collapse, be on the look-out for splinters from badly maintained boxes, benches and floors.

Always make sure that your exercise area is quite clear of equipment you are not using.

3

*Perfect facilities. This is the new British national training gymnasium at Lilleshall National Sports Centre.*

# Clothing

If your practice room is reasonably warm, you will need only the simplest of clothing for gymnastics. Leotards are ideal for girls, and vest and shorts for boys.

If there is any difficulty in keeping warm, thermal tights and a tracksuit top or sweater can be worn by either sex. Whatever you choose to wear must allow you to move freely, while not being so loose and floppy that it gets in the way while you are practising. Sweatshirts, sweaters and T-shirts which fall over your head when you turn upside down should be avoided! Tracksuit tops should always be zipped up.

Warming up effectively before trying gymnastics routines is really most important, and a track suit or jogging suit which will retain the body heat you generate during your preliminary exercises is ideal. Maintaining this body heat is particularly important when muscles are being stretched.

### Clothing points

- Tie long hair back. It's no fun performing a backward roll if your hair gets trapped under your hands!

- Clothing with buckles or similar kinds of fasteners must be avoided. Landing on a buckle can result in painful bruises, and when you progress to pairs work, there is also the danger of injury to your partner.

- Leave jewellery at home, and don't wear a watch either. Gymnastics and watches don't mix!

- In all gymnastics exercises, you have to show complete body control, and this includes your toes! You should perform in bare feet to start with, later progressing to specially made gymnastics shoes if you wish.

# Learning gymnastics skills

Most gymnastics skills, especially the more complicated ones, can be learned safely by working in stages. These stages gradually build up into the whole exercise, just as words build up into a sentence. It is important that each stage is mastered before you move on to the next one. There are no short cuts: apart from the need to progress safely, if you rush through the stages you will almost certainly pick up bad habits which will be very difficult to correct later.

# 3
# Basic shapes and positions

All sports have a language of their own, and gymnastics is no different. It is necessary to learn the special names given to particular body shapes and positions. Here are some of these, with brief explanations of how to show them correctly. Note the attention to detail; for example, the feet are held in the pointed position even during very simple exercises. Try to develop the habit of automatically adding *style* to your performance, right from the beginning.

### Front, side and back support

4

Whichever support position you are holding, your body and head should be in a straight line, without sagging or arching. For maximum strength and stability, the shoulders should be directly above your hands.

### Straddle stand and straddle jump

5

*Straddle stand*

In both the straddle stand and the straddle jump, you should keep your legs straight and wide apart. The back is also kept straight, and there is no bend at the waist.

*Straddle jump*

### Tuck and pike

These shapes are made by bending your body at the waist. In the tuck, you also bend your knees, but for the pike they are held straight.

In both cases, see how the ankles and knees are kept tight together and the toes are pointed.

*Tuck*

*Pike*

## Posture and body tension

You can't just rush into gymnastics without getting your body ready for the demands you are going to make upon it. In particular, you will find that your *trunk* needs special care and preparation.

The upper body is connected to the lower part by the spine, which is very flexible, and allows you to bend and twist in all directions. This flexibility is controlled by *body tension*, which is achieved by strengthening your stomach and back muscles and "teaching" them how to work correctly. Body tension is essential for two purposes: to stop all movement when necessary, for example during balances, and to provide the strength to protect the lower back from stress when jumping or landing.

In photo 9, the gymnasts are demonstrating the effect weak back and stomach muscles have on the back and front support positions. You won't sag like this if you have taught your muscles to hold your body correctly.

9

The next two pictures (10 and 11) show a gymnast landing from a jump off a low box. Look at the shape of the gymnast's back in each picture. Which do you think is safe? The landing with a curved back is the one which could lead to damage: it is similar to the shape in the example of poor front support in photo 9. If your spine tends to take up this posture, you need to develop better body tension — this will improve steadily as you progress. The exercises described in the next chapter will help.

10

11

*Don't let your back sag on landing: keep it straight, as in the photo on the right (11).*

# 4

# Warming up

The warm-up prepares your body for action and helps your mind to co-ordinate the action. It is a vital part of every training or practice session. As mentioned earlier, extra clothing should be worn to retain the heat generated by the warm-up activities. This is particularly important during the stretching exercises.

Warm-up need not be boring! Often all the members of a class will warm up together under the direction of the teacher or coach. The routine often contains games and partner activities which are a fun way of achieving the physical preparation required.

If you do have to exercise alone, try a routine such as this:

## Opening activity

This is where you prepare your body for full action by getting the blood flowing freely around it through using the large muscle groups.

- Start with jogging, skipping and side-stepping
- Build up to a more rapid combination of all three
- Now try repeated jumps on and off a bench or low box
- Add fast on-the-spot sprinting ...
- and some high-stepping runs.
- Finally, try some skipping.

You should finish this part of the warm-up feeling quite hot and breathing heavily.

**Note for coaches:** Games of "tag", and races down the hall and back, are good for groups.

# Stretching

This part of the session concentrates on the various parts of the body in turn, carefully taking each joint through its full range of movement. There are many stretching exercises which may be used for the ankles, hips, spine and shoulders, and a few are shown here. It is very important that the joints and muscles should be "coaxed" through their full range of movement. Use only *gentle* pressure, and avoid jerking and other harsh movements.

### Stretching exercises for ankles and legs

1 Sit on the floor and circle your ankles, so that your big toes make the biggest possible circles. Move only your feet and ankles, keeping the rest of your legs still.

12

2 Kneel down, keeping your ankles together: now lift your knees a little way off the floor. When you do this, you will find that it is natural to "point" your toes as you do in most gymnastics exercises.

13

3 Stand up straight. Keep your feet flat on the floor and bend your knees so that they go as far ahead of your toes as possible without your heels lifting off the floor. No cheating as in Figure 14 — keep those heels on the ground!

14

4 When you have finished stretching your ankles, sit on the floor and loosen them off by relaxing and shaking them as if trying to shake off a pair of shoes.

## Stretching thighs and hips

A good range of movement in the hip joints is a great advantage in gymnastics. Photos 15 and 16 show excellent flexibility in the forward/backward range of movement (splits) and in the sideways range (side splits).

**15**

**16**

5 Kneel down on one knee, and slide your front foot forward until you feel some stretch on the back of the leg. Now support your weight by putting your hands on the floor. Hold this position for about three seconds, making sure that the heel of your back foot is towards the ceiling and that the foot has not been allowed to roll inwards. Repeat, with the other foot at the front.

6 Take up the straddle-stand position, then slowly move your feet further and further apart until you feel the muscles on the inside of your legs starting to stretch. Hold this position briefly, then put your hands on the floor and sit down in a wide straddle sit. Finally, reach as far forward along the floor as possible, then relax and gently try to put your tummy on the floor.

**17**

7 After stretching your hips, a gentle jog on the spot will help loosen the muscles off again.

### Stretching the spine

Although your spine is capable of a vast range of movement, it must be treated very carefully. During warm-up it must be flexed forwards, backwards and sideways, as well as twisted. Spine exercises *must* be done steadily and without straining.

8 Lie face-down on the floor, with your hands under your shoulders. Gently press up until your arms are straight, but keep your hips on the floor. Lower your chest down to the floor again and repeat the action several times.

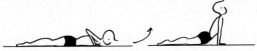

**18**

9 Turn on to your back and tuck up tightly. Rock backwards and forwards, keeping your back rounded as much as possible.

**19**

10 Sit on the floor with your legs a little way apart and your hands on the top of your head. Reach forwards and try to touch your right knee with your left elbow without taking your hands off your head, then repeat the stretch with the other elbow and knee. If you feel an uncomfortable stretch in the back of your legs, try bending your knees a little more. As you begin to loosen up, you can put more twist into your spine by spreading your legs further apart.

**20**

11 Lie on your back and place your hands palm-downwards on the floor, then press your whole body up off the floor until it is arched upwards. This is the *bridge* position.

**21**

### Shoulder stretching

A good range of movement in the shoulders is vital for many skills such as the handstand and the backward roll.

12 With your hands a little more than shoulder-width apart (or further apart if necessary), grasp a stick and hold it out in front of you. Keeping your arms straight, raise the stick up and over your head, and carry on until it is behind your back. Next, still keeping your arms straight, bring it slowly back in front of your body again. The distance apart of the hands should be adjusted so that you can perform the exercise without undue strain as the stick passes over your head. You should perform the exercise without releasing your grip or having to shrug your shoulders one at a time. Instead of a stick, you can use a piece of rope or a towel, pulled tight. The exercise should be repeated 15 to 20 times.

22

# Basic gymnastics skills

After stretching, you should introduce basic gymnastics skills to help you learn different body shapes and strengthen the muscles needed to maintain these shapes. The activities may first be practised separately and then combined into a short sequence or routine. This is still part of the warm-up.

When performing the activities as a short routine, each position should be held quite still for a few seconds before moving on to the next one. You must concentrate hard and make sure that good form is maintained all the time, especially when moving from one shape to another. All these exercises are good for developing the muscles you need for good body tension.

1 Lie flat on your back with your hands on your thighs. Keep your arms straight and slide your fingers down your legs until they *just* touch your knee-caps. Easy. Now round your back and try to put your chin on your chest; hold the position for as long as you can. Not quite so easy ... This is called the "dished" shape.

2 Roll over onto your front and stretch your arms above your head. Keep your legs straight and your feet tight together. Raise your chest and legs off the floor so that your back is arched and you are resting on your tummy. Hold this position for as long as you can.

*Once you can hold these positions for more than a few seconds, try rocking backwards and forwards while holding the shape tightly.*

3 Crouch down on a mat with your hands flat on the floor. Keeping your hands on the floor and your knees bent and tightly together, spring into the air, raising your seat as high as possible. Try to keep your feet off the floor for as long as you can. If you get high enough, you will find that you are well on the way to developing a handstand.

4 Sit on the floor with your legs straight out in front of you, toes pointed, and knees and ankles tightly together. Round your back and roll smoothly backwards until your toes are pointing towards the ceiling, then roll forwards to the sitting position again. Repeat several times.

23

## Building a sequence

If you join several of these warm-up exercises together, you can easily build a sequence which will very soon begin to look like a proper gymnastics performance. Try to do each part of the sequence *perfectly*. You should hold all the still positions for about three seconds:

1 From a good standing position, jump as high as you can: stretch while in the air and then land as lightly as possible. Immediately crouch down and shoot your feet backwards into a strong front-support position.

2

2  Turn through the side-support to the back-support
   position — remembering to hold each position for a
   few seconds — and lower yourself from back
   support to sitting with your legs straight. Then
   reach forwards to touch your legs as far down as
   possible.

**25**

3  Slowly stretch out your body again until you are
   lying flat on your back; bend your legs until your
   feet are flat on the floor, and put your hands flat on
   the floor by your ears. Now slowly push up into a
   bridge position. Hold this shape, then slowly lower
   yourself down and stretch out so that you are again
   lying on your back with your hands above your
   head.

**26**

4  Tighten your tummy muscles until you are in the
   "dished" shape. Hold this position, then stretch
   your arms above your head and at the same time
   roll over to balance on your tummy. Lower your
   legs and chest to the floor and put your hands flat
   on the floor by your shoulders. Straighten your
   arms so that you raise your chest as high as
   possible, but keep your hips on the floor.

**27**

5 Keeping your arms straight, lift your hips as high as possible. Bend your knees, and squat with your feet between your hands. Immediately jump into a high stretched jump and land softly. Finally, straighten up into the good standing position you had at the start.

28

You will soon find that putting together a sequence of this type is great fun — warm-ups need not be at all boring!

29

*A class of keen young gymnasts warming up. A track-suit is ideal for retaining body heat during this stage of the session.*

# 5

# Learning rolls

Now gymnastics begins to get exciting. The rolls are probably the most important skills you have to learn if you are to progress with the sport. Once you start to turn your body over rapidly, or to spin around, you may find that you lose your sense of where you are: you become *disoriented*. This is not unusual, and after a little practice you will become familiar with the sensations produced and learn to use rolls as a normal and easy way of turning over in different directions — forwards, backwards and sideways.

Rolling is also a good way of dealing with awkward falls or landings. When moving quickly your body has a great deal of energy. In gymnastics you learn to control this energy, but sometimes, especially when learning a new skill, you will not be completely successful! A roll is often the best way of ending the action without hurting yourself, as is seen throughout judo. Rolls are also used for this purpose in many other sports — for example, after a fall at speed on the hockey field, or when diving to save a goal at soccer — so practising rolls in gymnastics could prove useful on the sports field too.

Maybe you can already do some of these rolls. Children often learn to "turn somersaults" without any help from adults. But remember that there is a lot of difference between turning over with your arms and legs flopping all over the place, and the smooth action and perfect body posture which good gymnastic rolls demand.

## Forward roll

Start by rocking forwards and backwards in a tucked shape. Keep your back rounded and your knees tucked up to your chest. Try to rock smoothly from seat and feet to shoulders and back again (see Figure 30).

**30**

*Rocking forwards and backwards*

Once you can rock easily in a straight line, you can try to get into the roll. The simplest way is from the position shown in photo 31.

**31**

Crouch down with your knees well apart, and put your hands on the floor close to your feet. Look through your legs and try to see the ceiling. As your head goes between your legs, allow yourself to tip over into the roll, lowering your shoulders to the floor and keeping your head well tucked in.

If you have trouble at first going completely over, try starting from a kneeling position on a low box top or bench. Place your hands on the floor close to the box top or bench. Now tuck your chin onto your chest. Lift your seat in the air above your hands, and at the same time bend your arms and lower your shoulders onto the mat. Allow yourself to roll over and tuck up as in the rocking exercise. It is important that your shoulders take your body weight: the back of your head may brush the mat, but no weight must be taken on it.

**32**

*A forward roll starting from a low box top or bench*

An alternative method is to bend over a low beam and put your hands on the floor immediately under the beam or close to the apparatus.

**33**

You can control the speed with which you enter the roll by lifting your legs and allowing your thighs to slide off the apparatus. At the same time, duck your head, bend your arms and lower your shoulders to the floor. As your feet leave the support, tuck up and roll forwards as in the rocking exercise. At first you may not roll fast enough to go right over. Don't worry — get a partner to help by gently pulling you forwards as you rock to the exit position. This way you will soon get the feel of the movement.

**34**

Once you have got the feel of the roll, you can polish up your style. Let's go through the whole exercise again:

The "correct" way of starting a forward roll is by crouching with your ankles and knees together and your arms stretched out in front of you. Tip forwards to put your hands on the floor ...

**35**

... and push with your feet by straightening your legs strongly. At the same time, take your weight on your hands, duck your head and lower your shoulders to the floor. The strong push with your legs will propel you into the roll. As your feet leave the floor, simply tuck up tightly and allow the roll to continue.

36

All that remains is to polish up your exit: take your hands from your shins and reach forwards. Keep your heels as close to your seat as possible, and allow the roll to continue until you feel your weight on your feet again. Finish off by standing up smoothly with your arms at your sides. Your feet and knees must stay tightly together throughout the roll.

37

**Note for coaches:** If your pupils are having difficulty in rolling fast enough to get back on their feet, they will find it much easier if they roll down a slope. The simplest method is to place a mat over a vaulting board.

38

*A backward roll made easier with the aid of a vaulting board*

26

# Sideways roll

As with the forward roll, the most important aspect of this roll is the shape of the body in the middle of the roll. Photo 39 shows the shape to take up for the tucked sideways roll. See how the elbows are tight into the groin area so that the roll can be completed without your arms becoming trapped under your body.

**39**

The sideways roll is easy. Here's how to do one to the left:

Start by kneeling down with your arms extended level with your shoulders. Now drop your left arm across in front of your body, then move your seat down to your heels. Dip your left shoulder and allow yourself to tip sideways into the roll. As you start to roll, take up the shape shown in photo 39. Continue smoothly until you have rolled onto your shins again, then finally straighten up into the starting position. Easy! Now drop your right arm and repeat the process to the right, so that you roll back to where you started.

**40**

You will soon be able to make variations on this roll, and two are illustrated below. Always remember to keep your back rounded during all these rolls: don't let it go flat onto the floor.

**41**

**42**

# Backward roll

Start the backward roll by rocking forwards and backwards, as for the forward roll. However, as you roll backwards, place your hands flat on the floor by the side of your head. They should be shoulder-width apart, with the thumbs pointing towards your ears, as Figure 43 shows. Notice that the toes, elbows and seat are all pointing towards the ceiling.

 **43**

Finish the backward roll by pushing strongly with your arms as you rock backwards. This will lift your shoulders off the floor and allow your head to come between your arms. It will also ensure that your hips are high enough to bring your feet — not your knees — to the floor. Make sure that the tucked shape is retained until your feet are on the floor.

**Note for coaches:** The backward roll is not quite as easy as the forward one at first, and assistance from a coach will help. Photo 44 shows the best way to assist, by lifting the hips.

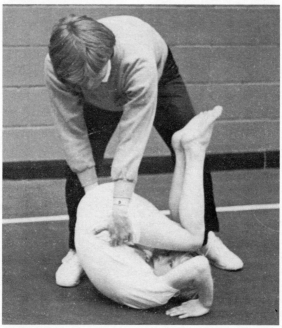 **44**

# Circle straddle roll

This roll is fun to do and very easy to learn, provided that you take care with your body shape and direction of rolling. Sit in a wide straddle position and put your hands on your legs just below your knees. For a roll to the left, start by lifting your right leg off the floor and tipping on to your left side. Keep your body bent at the hips, and roll across your back until your right side is on the floor; your left leg will now be in the air. Hold the bend at the hips and bring the left leg back down to the floor. You will now be sitting in a straddle position, but facing in the opposite direction, as Figure 45 shows.

45

## Circle straddle checklist

- Keep legs straight and wide apart.
- Keep bent at the waist.
- Make sure that the roll is started by going sideways.

# 6

# Balances

Balances are an essential part of gymnastics. At first, you will find great satisfaction in mastering the easier balances, before progressing to the more difficult ones. Eventually you will be able to hold even these with perfect control.

Here we introduce some simple balances in which your body will be upside-down – *inverted* balances.

## Shoulder balance

This balance is simple, so you can concentrate on style early on: try for a stretched body with good tension – your shoulders, hips and feet should be in a vertical line, with your legs held tightly together.

There are three forms of shoulder balance:

● In the simplest, you support your hips by stabilising them with your hands while keeping your elbows on the floor.

● It is slightly more difficult to hold the position by stretching your arms out and pressing down on the floor behind your back with your hands.

● The hardest shoulder balance is with your arms stretched out along the floor above your head. You will find that it is surprisingly difficult to maintain a straight, vertical shape in this balance.

46

# Headstand

This is a popular balance, and easy to learn. Start by kneeling on a mat, and place your hands on the floor about shoulder-width apart. Put the front part of the top of your head on the floor so that a triangular shape is made, with your hands forming the base of the triangle.

Now straighten your legs, and, while pressing strongly on the floor, walk in on your toes until your seat is over your head. Don't allow your back to become rounded, and take care not to roll onto the *back* of your head, or you will simply go over into a forward roll. Once your seat is over your head, straighten your back and tuck your knees to your chest. Ensure that your toes are pointing towards the ceiling, and that there is weight on your hands as well as on your head.

As soon as you can hold a tucked headstand easily, try straightening your legs slowly into the full headstand. As you straighten your legs, you will have to move your hips back slightly in order to maintain weight on your hands. As with the shoulder balance, you should be aiming at a clean body line and good body tension.

*A selection of headstands*

*A trio of good shoulder balances. You will find that the one on the right of the three is hard to achieve.*

**Note for coaches:** When your gymnasts can perform a competent headstand, encourage them to vary it by changing the position of their legs, as well as trying different methods of moving into or out of the balance. Photo 49 (page 31) shows a selection of headstands.

# Handstand

The handstand balance is a lot more difficult than anything you have tried up to now! It requires strength in the arms and shoulders, and very good body tension.

### Walking up a wall
The easiest way to learn the handstand and help build up the strength required is by "walking up a wall". Kneel down on a mat with your back to a wall. Place your hands on the floor by the side of your knees, and simply start walking up the wall behind you while taking your weight on your hands. The higher up the wall you walk, the closer you get to the handstand. If at any time you feel the need to come down, duck your head, bend your arms and push off from the wall with your feet, which will send you into a forward roll.

Practise this until you can walk up the wall almost to a handstand, and then "walk" in towards the wall on your arms until your hands, shoulders, hips and feet are all in a vertical line. Always use a forward roll to come out of the handstand against a wall.

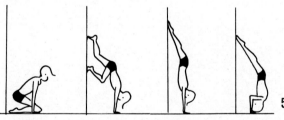

50

While practising the handstand, keep your arms straight and look at your hands all the time.

### Kicking to handstand
When you have got the feel of the handstand by walking up the wall, it is time to try kicking into the position. Stand facing the wall with your arms stretched over your head. Take a long lunge step forward, and bring your chest down to the bent knee. Place your hands on the floor, about 300 mm (1 ft) away from the wall, and swing the stretched leg up over your head. At the same time push hard on the floor by straightening

your bent leg and swinging it up so that both legs rest against the wall.

51

Once you are able to kick to handstand against the wall, you can start practising holding the balance. Press very hard against the floor with your fingers and, with just a tiny push from the wall with your feet, straighten your body and keep it stiff in a vertical line. Try to hold this position for as long as possible without your feet touching the wall.

Finally, try kicking to handstand without using a wall at all. You won't get it right at first, but keep trying! If you start to fall over the top, *either* bend your arms, duck your head and go into a forward roll, as you did when practising "walking up the wall", *or* take one hand off the floor and turn your body to put your feet on the floor to one side.

In a good handstand, you will see excellent body tension and a very straight body line. There should be no arch in the back at all.

**52**

*Super style shown in a beautifully held handstand*

*Most beginners find that the cartwheel is easy to master if they start by learning over a bench.*

34

# 7

# The cartwheel

The cartwheel is one of the most common gymnastics exercises, but it is often done very badly. The trick is to get the hand and foot pattern correct from the start. This is a lot easier if you perform your first cartwheels over a bench.

**Note for coaches:** The instructions given below are for a gymnast who finds it easiest to lead with the left foot. Those who naturally lead with the right foot should read "right" for "left" and vice versa.

Follow these steps to learn a good cartwheel which will become a useful linking action when you are putting together a gymnastics performance:

1 Start correctly, standing with feet together facing the bench and about one metre (3 ft) away from it.

2 Step forward with your left foot, and place your left hand on the near side of the bench first, opposite your left knee.

3 Place your right hand on the far side of the bench, directly opposite the left one.

4 Swing your right leg over the bench and place your right foot on the floor in line with your hands.

5 Now swing your left leg over the bench. Just before your left foot comes down to the floor, take your left hand off the bench. This will allow your body to turn slightly so that your left foot can be grounded in line with your right foot and beyond it.

6 Finish by taking your right hand off the bench, and stretch up into a "star" shape.

7 Check that you have turned correctly during the last part of the cartwheel: you should now be facing the wall which was on your *right* when you faced the bench to start.

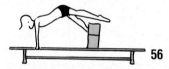
So far you have got the sequence right, but your body is not yet completely inverted halfway through. Here is the way to achieve this:

● Place something soft, such as a foam cushion, on the bench where your legs pass over it. You then have to cartwheel without kicking the obstacle off, and *without letting your action become sloppy*. Keep cartwheeling, but steadily pile up the cushions until they are about 600 mm (2 ft) high.

**56**

The next stage involves placing your hands on the floor instead of on the bench. After your practice on the bench, you should be able to do this quite easily, but a little support may help. Continue to use a chalked line as a guide.

**57**

*A little support will build confidence when you transfer to the floor.*

Don't rush the last stages of development. Make sure that your cartwheel is remaining on the straight line, and that your starting and finishing positions are accurate. Just work steadily at improving your style until you are able to keep it completely vertical every time. Photo 58 shows what you should be aiming at: see how the gymnast's back is straight, not arched, and her legs are in a very wide straddle shape.

58

# 8

# Vaulting

Every vault has a take-off and a landing, and it may appear strange to describe the landing first. However, for safety you must master the technique for a correct landing before you can progress to the more exciting parts of vaulting.

## Safe landing

Start practising vault landings by stretch-jumping from a box-top or bench. Stretch your body in the air, but try to land as softly as you can. You should come down on the balls of your feet, and bend your ankles, knees and hips slightly. A good landing will be very quiet and well balanced. When you get it right, there should be no need to adjust the position of your feet to keep your balance once you are on the ground.

**59**

Don't bend your knees too much: you might damage your knee joints.

As you gain more control of your landings, you can increase the height from which you jump. You can also add some variety by making different shapes in the air before landing. Tucked jumps and star jumps are popular, but do experiment with other shapes of your own.

*Don't let your knees bend too much when you land (photo 62): photo 63 shows just the right amount of flex.* ➡

38

***Above:*** *A star jump*
***Below:*** *Leaving the horse in a tucked position*

# Starting to vault

You need to practise some basic exercises on the ground before flying through the air! Try these:

### The bunny jump
Crouch down on a mat with your arms behind you. Now swing your arms forwards, and spring along the mat to land on your hands. As soon as your hands touch, you must thrust strongly against the floor and lift your head and shoulders up. If these two actions are timed correctly, you should "bounce" off your hands. As this happens, bend your knees and bring your feet back to the floor. You have to push *really strongly* with your hands, so that they are off the ground with your arms in front of you *before* your feet are back on the ground.

64

> **Note for coaches:** If the bunny jump is done correctly, there will be two moments when neither hands nor feet are touching the ground — first during the spring from feet to hands, and then after the thrust from hands to feet.

### The bunny jump to straddle stand
You can try this variation of the bunny jump by keeping your legs straight after the initial jump. As you make the thrust with your hands, spread your legs so that you land in the straddle-stand position with your arms stretched out forwards.

65

Now to add some height to the exercises... The next activities are performed on a box top.

### The squat-on
When you do a bunny jump onto a vaulting box, it is called a *squat-on*. Try doing a few onto the end of the box top. Put plenty of effort into your jumps — especially into the push-off with your hands, so that you

end up standing in a good position on the box. Your hands must have left the top before your feet land on it.

As your confidence increases, the box should be raised until you are able to squat-on to three or four sections, depending on your age and height. This will need a short approach run of two or three paces. Once you can do this easily, without running the risk of catching your feet and toppling forwards head first, spring up from the side of the box, so that you approach it crosswise. Practise this until you can squat-on and immediately stretch-jump off to a correct landing.

When you jump down after each squat-on, don't forget to practise a correct vault landing each time.

### The through vault

It is easy now to turn your squat-on into a through vault. From a slightly faster approach, say four or five paces, use the same strong thrust from the hands, but instead of landing with your feet on the box, allow them to pass over and stretch for the floor on the far side. You will soon be vaulting cleanly over the box with one smooth action.

It is important that you have someone to support you for the first few attempts. Photo 67 shows the best way to do this.

*The vaulting board has helped the gymnast to get plenty of height for this through vault.*

### The straddle vault

The next vault to master is the *straddle*. Jump up onto the box using the same approach as for the through vault, but land on top in the straight-legged straddle position. This is called *straddling-on*. For the first few attempts at each height of box, you need to have a helper standing on the far side in case you should fall forwards.

When straddling-on, your hands must have left the top before your feet land on it. Once you are on the top, bring your feet together before jumping off.

The next step, the complete straddle vault, will follow quite naturally if you increase the speed of your approach slightly and continue over the box without pausing at the top.

Once you have learned the vaults over the low box, and your landings are secure, then you can progress to a higher box and vault over this with the aid of a vaulting board. Remember — each time you increase the height of the box, you must have a supporter to help you through the first few attempts.

**70**

*Assistance for a straddle vault. See how the gymnast
has placed her hands on the far side of the box so that
she will clear it easily.*

# 9

## Competitive gymnastics

So far you have learned some simple gymnastics, which may seem very different from the dazzling performances you see on the television screen. However, you will have learned to perform accurately and with good style, and that is the basis for success in competition at any level. You cannot learn advanced gymnastics solely from a book — you must have a trainer or coach for that — but we can give you an idea of what the judges will be looking for if you do take up gymnastics as a competitive sport.

# Levels of competition

There are two main pathways into competition: open gymnastics clubs, and your country's schools gymnastics association.

For juniors, the schools organisations offer a level of competition designed specifically with the school gym club in mind; this is slightly less demanding than the open type. In Great Britain, the British Schools Gymnastics Association (BSGA) organises a whole series of competition opportunities, which are based on the award schemes of the British Amateur Gymnastics Association (BAGA).

Most competition gymnasts follow the usual route of competing at club, city, regional, and eventually national level.

# Elements of competition

In artistic gymnastics, men and women compete separately, and both the tasks and the apparatus are different — only the vault and the floor exercises on a mat twelve metres (39 ft) square feature in both.

### Women's competition

- Asymmetric bars
- Balance beam
- Floor
- Vaulting horse

### Men's competition

- Floor
- High bar
- Parallel bars
- Pommel horse
- Rings
- Vaulting horse

Although fluid movement and style are still extremely important for men, some of the men's exercises — particularly those on the rings — put more emphasis on pure strength than the women's exercises do.

*Alexander Tumilovich (USSR), performing the men's floor exercises*

# The basis of scoring

Scoring gymnastics performances is a complicated business — especially so in international competitions: judging gymnastic quality of movement and technical precision is a matter of informed opinion which is limited by very strict guidelines. It is quite unlike judging who gets to a line first. Judges have to decide whether a relatively simple vault which is exquisitely executed is really better than a daring and complex one which has a few rough edges to it.

In order to provide a firm basis from which to judge, the international governing body for gymnastics, the Fédération Internationale de Gymnastique (FIG), has laid down a detailed set of rules which are revised at four-yearly intervals. These are called the *Code of Points*.

When a gymnast competes, the score for each routine is compiled from a number of clearly-defined factors:

● **Difficulty** The difficulty rating of each element (individual skill) is set out in the *Code of Points*. To gain maximum points for difficulty, the routine must include a set number of skills of particular difficulty ratings.

● **Special requirements** In some cases, gymnasts may be required to include specific types of movement in their routines. For example, men on the high bar are required to include the skill of releasing the bar and catching it again.

● **Combination** This is how the routine is put together, including how the apparatus is used. For example, the floor exercise should show such things as good use of the whole area, rhythm and harmony.

● **Execution** A gymnast should perform each skill perfectly: any falling short of perfection is penalised.

● **Bonus** There is also a special points allowance which may be added to a gymnast's score for performing skills that are particularly difficult, complex or unusual. These extra points may also be given for "virtuosity" — presenting the routine, or part of the routine, with extraordinary technical excellence.

As you can see, it is a highly skilled task to be an expert in all these areas and to be able to take them into account quickly as a routine progresses. It takes many years to build up the experience needed to become a judge at international level.

**72** *Rhythmic gymnastics is related to women's artistic gymnastics, and has been included in the Olympic Games since 1984. Here Bianca Panova of Bulgaria performs an intricate routine with the ribbon, one of the standard pieces of apparatus. The rules for competition and scoring differ from those in artistic gymnastics: difficulty, combination and execution are still important, however, with particular emphasis being placed on artistic aspects such as harmony and fluidity. Each routine is accompanied by a solo musical instrument, normally a piano.*

# 10

# The terms explained

Many gymnastics activities and exercises are named after the gymnast who first developed them or performed them in public. Here we indicate some of the commonest ones which you are likely to meet when watching televised gymnastics, and also explain the words which have a special meaning when applied to gymnastics. Where measurements are given, they are approximate.

**Amplitude** In gymnastics, *amplitude* is used to describe both the overall size of a movement and its completeness.

**Asymmetric bars** This apparatus is used by women gymnasts only. Two bars, each 2.4 m (8 ft) long, are mounted parallel but at different heights: one bar is 2.3 m (7 ft 6 in) from the ground, the other 1.5 m (5 ft). The separation between the bars may be adjusted to suit the individual gymnast.

*Svetlana Baitova (USSR) on the asymmetric bars*

**Beam** The beam is 100 mm (4 in) wide and 5 m (16 ft) long, with a flat upper surface. For competition the beam is 1.2 m (4 ft) above the ground.

*The beam demands poise and courage. This is Hana Runa, from Czechoslovakia.*

**Box** The box is a rectangular box-shaped form of *horse* with a padded top. It is constructed in layers about 220 mm (9 in) deep, enabling the height to be altered readily.

**Chalk** The chalk which gymnasts rub onto their hands is magnesium carbonate. It helps to prevent the bars becoming slippery, and allows a firm grip.

**Compulsory routine** In the Olympic Games and World Championships, the gymnasts are required to perform a compulsory exercise on each piece of apparatus. These routines are judged on quality of movement and technical excellence only.

**Element** Each individual identifiable part of a gymnastics performance is referred to as an *element*.

**Endo** The endo is a complicated high-bar exercise terminating in a handstand, named after the great Japanese gymnast Yukio Endo. It is *not* a vault in which everything goes wrong and the performer finishes up going end-over-end! (*Endo* is used in this latter sense in some other sports, such as BMX racing.)

**Flic-flac** A backward *handspring*.

**Handspring** A handspring consists of a complete forward turn of the body in which only the hands touch the floor or apparatus.

**Hecht** The hecht is the swallow-dive position, where the arms are outstretched and the legs and toes pointed.

**High bar** The high bar is used in men's gymnastics. It is mounted almost 3.5 m (12 ft) from the ground. The performer has to remain constantly in motion throughout the exercise sequence, which will include a wide variety of circling activities around the bar. Spectacular dismounts involving multiple aerial somersaults are usually a feature of a good high-bar routine.

75

*Peter Vidmar (USA) on the high bar*

**Hold** A hold is a position or balance which is deliberately held still. In competition, holds should be for a duration of three seconds.

**Horse** The horse is an apparatus with four legs and a strong padded body, used for vaulting. It owes its origin to the dummy horses upon which warriors used to practise mounting and fighting. In competitive gymnastics, women vault across the horse, and men vault along it. Men also perform exercises on the *pommel horse*, which has handles mounted on it in about the position where a saddle would fit.

*Right:* Ian Shelley (GB) attacks the horse.

*Below:* Andrew Morris (GB) on the pommel horse

**76**

**77**

**Kip** The kip is the action in which the gymnast moves from hanging beneath a bar with arms in tension, to balancing with the bar at hip-height and arms in compression. The kip is a common way of starting exercises on the bars.

**Mat** In everyday gymnastics, the mat is the padded covering on the floor. For competitive gymnasts it is an area twelve metres (39 ft) square upon which the *mat exercises* are performed.

**Parallel bars** The parallel bars are used only in men's gymnastics. The two bars are mounted level with each other, a little below head-height, and their spacing may be adjusted slightly to suit the competitor. In recent years, glassfibre-reinforced materials have been used in the construction of the bars, and this has helped the gymnasts to give ever more spectacular performances.

78

*Ian Shelley showing great strength and concentration on the parallel bars*

**Pike** The pike is the position in which the body is bent at the hips, with the legs remaining straight.

**Pommel horse** See *horse*.

**Rhythmic gymnastics** Rhythmic gymnastics takes the form of floor exercises to music. It is for female gymnasts only, and concentrates on dance and the manipulation of small items of apparatus such as hoop, ball, ribbon, rope or clubs. Somersaults and acrobatic skills are not allowed.

**79**

*Spain's Nuria Salido is one of the most graceful performers in rhythmic gymnastics.*

**Rings** The rings are used by men only. Two rings are suspended 2.5 m (just over 8 ft) from the ground, shoulder-width apart. The exercises call for great muscular strength in the arms and shoulders, coupled with extreme flexibility. (See photo 80 on page 54.)

**Round-off** A round-off is similar to a cartwheel, but the gymnast makes a quarter-turn of the body, brings the feet together, and lands travelling backwards. A round-off is usually the first skill performed in a floor routine as the gymnast goes into the first tumbling series.

**Salto** A somersault performed in flight.

**Scale** A balance on one leg.

**Sports acrobatics** Sports acrobatics is a form of gymnastics in which pairs or groups of up to four gymnasts perform routines consisting of balances and synchronised agilities linked with dance movements.

**Spotter** A spotter is someone who stands close to a horse or other apparatus in order to assist with support if necessary.

**Tinsica** The tinsica is a floor or beam skill similar to a cartwheel, except that the gymnast makes a quarter-turn at the end of the cartwheel so as to face the direction of travel.

**Trampoline** The trampoline consists of a stretched and sprung sheet of resilient material, used for aerial tumbling. *Trampolining* has developed into a distinct branch of gymnastics. Small trampolines, called *trampettes*, can be used as springboards.

**Tsukahara** The tsukahara is a vault in which the gymnast performs a half-turn, passing through the handstand position on top of the horse, and then immediately pushes off from the hands to complete the movement with a one-and-a-half-revolution backward somersault to the floor.

**Tuck** In the tuck position, the legs are bent at the knees, which are brought up to the chest. It allows a high speed of rotation during aerial somersaults.

**Yurchenko** The yurchenko is a vault similar to the tsukahara, except that the half-turn is produced by performing a *round-off* onto the board and then jumping backwards into the handstand position.

**80**

*The rings can demand great flexibility as well as strength. This is Sepp Zellwegger from Switzerland.*

# 11

# Award schemes

## Gymnastics proficiency awards

In Great Britain, the British Amateur Gymnastics Association offers a comprehensive series of award schemes for recreational gymnastics. Gymnasts of all ages can receive recognition of their progress, gaining badges and certificates as they reach specified performance levels. Incentive awards are available even for pre-school children, so it is possible to choose an appropriate starting rung at any point on the "performance ladder". Full details are available from the Technical Department of BAGA (see page 56). The national gymnastics associations in other countries provide similar awards.

## Coaching award schemes

The enormous demand for opportunities to participate in gymnastics has created a parallel demand for gymnastics coaches and teachers. BAGA has recognised this, and has a very comprehensive coach training and award system in operation. Teachers, interested parents, senior pupils, former gymnasts, sports leaders, and indeed anyone who would like to teach gymnastics skills, can receive training in the background knowledge and coaching techniques required. There is a demand in your area! Contact BAGA or your national gymnastics association.

# Useful addresses

## British Isles

British Amateur Gymnastics
   Association
Ford Hall
Lilleshall National Sports Centre
Nr Newport
Shropshire TF10 9NB

British Schools Gymnastics
   Association
26 Broom Acres
Sandhurst, Camberley
Surrey GU17 8PW

Irish Amateur Gymnastics
   Association
House of Sport
Long Mile Road
Dublin 12

Northern Ireland Amateur
   Gymnastics Association
House of Sport
Upper Malone Road
Belfast BT9 5LA

Scottish Amateur Gymnastics
   Association
8B Melville Street
Falkirk FK1 1HZ

Welsh Amateur Gymnastics
   Association
National Sports Centre
Sophia Gardens
Cardiff CF1 9SW

## Overseas

Australian Gymnastics Federation
2-6 Redwood Drive
Dingley
Victoria 3172

Canadian Gymnastics Federation
Suite 510
1600 James Naismith Drive
Gloucester
Ontario K1B 5N4

New Zealand Gymnastics
   Association
Suite 77A, Cashel Chambers
Christchurch 1

United States Gymnastics
   Federation
Pan American Plaza
Suite 300, 201 S Capitol
Indianapolis
Indiana 46225

## International

Fédération Internationale de Gymnastique
M. Max Bangerter, Secretary-General
Case Postale 16
CH-3250 Lyss
Switzerland